50 Shades of Said

And Other Common Verbs

RC Bonitz
Judy Roth

ISBN-13: 978-1494482749
ISBN-10: 1494482746

Cover Design by
Raman Bhardwaj
www.artistraman.com

ABOUT THE AUTHORS

RC Bonitz is a multi-published author of heartwarming love stories. A former sailor, he devotes his time to the craft of writing these days. RC and his wife are the loving parents of five children and twelve boisterous and wonderful grandchildren. You can reach RC at http://www.rcbonitz.com

Judy Roth is a writer who discovered a surprising love of editing. She now keeps one toe in the writing world but spends most of her time as a freelance editor and speaker. Judy and her husband are the proud parents of two strapping young men. You can reach Judy at http://www.judy-roth.com

RC and Judy have been critique partners for seventeen years. This is their first collaborative effort.

Table of Contents

<u>Introduction</u>

Using the appropriate word can make or break a scene. Often going simple is the best way, but sometimes something distinctive is required.

This little book contains more than 300 synonyms with definitions for three of the most commonly used verbs in fiction—SAID, WALKED and LOOKED.

We hope you find some useful alternatives to help you kick your writing up a notch.

Have Fun!

1

Alternatives for Said

A

Accuse: _To place blame._

Acknowledge: _To recognize the presence of another or agree with a statement._

Add: _To supply further information to an existing discussion._

Admit: _To concede or confess._

Admonish: _To gently disapprove._

Advise: _To warn or counsel._

Affirm: _To confirm, to agree in a positive manner._

Agree: _To concur._

Allege: _To claim a statement or incident is true._

Announce: *To declare in a formal manner.*

Answer: *To reply or respond.*

Approve: *To offer agreement or to endorse.*

Argue: *To give an opposite opinion, to disagree. Can be, but does not have to be in a confrontational or challenging tone.*

Ask: *To inquire.*

Assert: *To speak with conviction.*

Assure: *To offer a guarantee.*

Aver: *To insist.*

Avow: *To state confidently.*

B

Babble: *To speak excitedly and quickly. Or in the case of a small child to make unintelligible sounds.*

Banter: *To tease back and forth.*

Bark: *To speak sharply.*

Beg: *To plead.*

Bellow: *To speak very loudly and forcibly.*

Bleat: *To whimper.*

Blurt: *To speak impulsively, without thinking.*

Bluster: *To threaten or bluff with more confidence than conviction.*

Boom: *To speak loudly and often with authority.*

Break in: *To interrupt.*

Breathe: *To speak in a soft and airy manner.*

Bubble: *To speak quickly with excitement.*

C

Call: *To hail.*

Caution: *To warn.*

Chant: *To speak in a monotonous or repetitive manner, often in melodic tones.*

Chatter: *To prattle on.*

Cheer: *To give encouragement.*

Chide: *To gently scold.*

Chime in: *To add an uninvited statement or opinion to a conversation.*

Choke out: *To speak with difficulty.*

Chorus: *To agree with a previous statement or opinion. Two or more people speaking the same thing at the same time.*

Claim: *To allege or declare.*

Cluck: *To speak in a fawning manner.*

Coax: *To encourage agreement or action.*

Command: *To demand.*

Comment: *To make an observation or to remark.*

Complain: *To protest or grumble.*

Compliment: *To give praise or approval.*

Concede: *To give in.*

Conclude: *To call a halt.*

Concur: *To agree.*

Confess: *To admit.*

Confide: *To entrust another with information.*

Congratulate: *To express praise.*

Consent: *To give permission.*

Contend: *To argue for something.*

Continue: *To keep talking or follow through with a thought.*

Contradict: *To say the opposite.*

Correct: *To alter a conclusion or situation to make it accurate.*

Counter: *To offer an opposing or alternate opinion.*

Crow: *To brag or gloat.*

Cry: *To speak loudly and with emotion.*

D

Dare: *To goad.*

Declaim: *To proclaim arrogantly.*

Declare: *To announce or proclaim as fact.*

Demand: *To insist.*

Describe: *To explain or depict an event or scene.*

Differ: *To offer an opposing idea or opinion.*

Disagree: *To offer an opposing idea or opinion.*

Disclose: *To reveal or make known.*

Divulge: *To reveal or make known.*

Drawl: *To draw out in a slow or relaxed style of speech.*

E

Echo: *To repeat or imitate.*

Emphasize: *To stress a point or opinion.*

Enunciate: *To articulate slowly and distinctly.*

Exclaim: *To speak loudly and vehemently.*

Explain: *To clarify.*

F

Fib: *To tell a small lie.*

Finish: *To end a statement or conversation.*

Fret: *To worry or fuss.*

Fume: *To speak in anger.*

G

Gab: *To chat, usually about inconsequential matters.*

Gloat: *To revel with patronizing superiority.*

Greet: *To welcome or acknowledge someone.*

Groan: *To speak in a moan of pain or displeasure.*

Growl: *To speak angrily.*

Grumble: *To mutter in anger or displeasure.*

Grunt: *To speak in a short and angry tone.*

Guess: *To deduce or suppose.*

Gush: *To prattle on overenthusiastically.*

H

Harrumph: *To convey a self-important opinion in a gruff manner.*

Hold forth: *To pontificate.*

Hint: *To give a small amount of information or intimate.*

Hiss: *To speak disapprovingly in a whisper.*

Holler: *To shout.*

Hypothesize: *To theorize.*

I

Imitate: *To copy or mimic.*

Implore: *To plead.*

Imply: *To infer or suggest.*

Indicate: *To specify or show.*

Infer: *To imply or surmise.*

Inform: *To give information.*

Inquire: *To ask.*

Insist: *To demand.*

Instruct: *To teach or command.*

Interject: *To interrupt a speaker with words.*

Interrupt: *To stop someone from speaking.*

Intone: *To speak in a flat, dull tone.*

J

Jeer: *To taunt or ridicule.*

Jest: *To speak in a joking or lighthearted manner.*

Joke: *To tell a story meant to bring laughter. To jest or speak in a lighthearted manner.*

K

Kid: *To joke or speak in a lighthearted manner.*

L

Lament: *To speak with regret or sorrow.*

Lie: *To speak untruthfully.*

Lisp: *To speak with one's tongue between one's teeth.*

M

Maintain: *To affirm or reaffirm a point of view.*

Marvel: *To wonder.*

Mention: *To point out or comment.*

Mimic: *To copy or imitate.*

Moan: *To lament in a low and prolonged tone.*

Mock: *To copy or repeat in a ridiculing manner.*

Mumble: *To speak quietly and indistinctly.*

Murmur: *To speak softly and gently.*

Mutter: *To speak quietly and indistinctly. Connotes displeasure.*

N

Nag: *To pester in a scolding and repetitive manner.*

Note: *To point out or remind.*

O

Object: *To dispute or disagree.*

Observe: *To take note of.*

Offer: *To present or suggest something (as a possibility).*

Order: *To command.*

P

Pant: *To struggle for breath while speaking.*

Peep: *To speak briefly in a weak voice.*

Pipe up: *To interrupt or chime in.*

Plead: *To beg.*

Point out: *To convey an opinion with emphasis.*

Praise: *To offer approval.*

Prattle: *To chatter on or gossip.*

Proclaim: *To announce loudly or emphatically.*

Prod: *To urge.*

Promise: *To offer a guarantee or warning.*

Pronounce: *To declare formally.*

Propose: *To suggest or recommend.*

Protest: *To object.*

Purr: *To speak in a soft, self-assured, seductive tone.*

Push: *To urge or prod.*

Q

Quaver: *To speak tremulously.*

Question: *To raise doubts about another's statement or request information.*

Quip: *To speak in a brief joking manner.*

Quote: *To use another's words with attribution.*

R

Rant: *To go on a tirade.*

Rasp: *To speak in a gravely or strained voice.*

Reason: *To try to convince with logic.*

Reassure: *To ease someone's anxiety.*

Recall: *To remember.*

Refute: *To disagree or dispute.*

Relate: *To convey facts.*

Rejoin: *To respond.*

Remark: *To comment on.*

Remember: *To recall.*

Remind: *To bring to one's attention again.*

Remonstrate: *To take issue with.*

Repeat: *To say more than once.*

Reply: *To answer.*

Report: *To announce, as with news.*

Request: *To ask for something.*

Respond: *To reply.*

Resume (speaking): *To pick up a thought and continue speaking.*

Retort: *To give a snappish reply.*

Reveal: *To let slip a secret.*

Roar: *To shout loudly and with great intensity.*

S

Sass: *To respond with impudent or disrespectful back-talk.*

Scold: *To chastise.*

Scream: *To yell.*

Seethe: *To speak with controlled fury.*

Shout: *To call loudly.*

Shriek: *To give a shrill, loud, sharp cry.*

Shrill: *To speak in a high-pitched anxious or angry tone.*

Sing out: *To cry out.*

Snap: *To speak or respond curtly.*

Snarl: *To growl or speak harshly with disdain or a threat.*

Sneer: *To speak with contempt or derision.*

Snivel: *To whine.*

Sob: *To express overwhelming sadness.*

Soothe: *To calm or ease another's feelings.*

Speak: *To say.*

Speculate: *To guess with some information.*

Spit out: *To speak sharply, with vehemence.*

Splutter: *To speak in a confused, stumbling fashion, usually as a result of surprise.*

Sputter: *To speak in a confused, stumbling fashion, usually as a result of surprise.*

Squeak: *To speak with a small voice, often a result of surprise or embarrassment.*

Squeal: *To cry out with overwhelming excitement or to spill the beans.*

Stammer: *To speak in a stumbling fashion, usually as a result of surprise or uncertainty.*

State: *To speak with emphasis or certainty.*

Storm: *To rage, speak angrily.*

Stress: *To speak with emphasis.*

Stutter: *To speak with difficulty.*

Suggest: *To recommend or hint at.*

Surmise: *To guess at or figure out.*

T

Taunt: *To tease nastily or viciously.*

Tease: *To say playfully or with humor and an edge.*

Tell: *To say, inform.*

Tempt: *To entice.*

Threaten: *To give warning in the form of a promise to harm.*

Trail off: *To let one's voice fade away.*

U

Urge: *To encourage, prod.*

Utter: *To say.*

V

Venture: *To offer, as a thought or idea.*

Vocalize: *To talk or sing out.*

Voice: *To speak.*

Volunteer: *To offer ideas, opinions, or services.*

Vow: *To promise or threaten.*

W

Wail: *To cry plaintively.*

Warn: *To alert someone to possible harm or disaster.*

Weep: *To cry mournfully.*

Whimper: *To cry out in a sad or wistful manner.*

Whine: *To complain or gripe in an unappealing, self-pitying fashion.*

Whisper: *To speak very softly.*

Wonder: *To contemplate with curiosity or astonishment.*

Worry: *To speak anxiously or with apprehension.*

Y

Yell: *To shout or demand attention.*

Alternatives for Walk

A

Amble: _To walk or wander casually with no need to rush._

Approach: _To move closer to._

B

Barrel: _To rush forward in a determined way or force one's way through._

Bounce: _To jog or pop up and down._

Bowl: _To move quickly with abandon._

Burst: _To move explosively or start quickly._

C

Careen: _To move or fall with limited control._

Clamber: *To hastily climb with feet and hands, usually in a difficult situation.*

Clump: *To walk with heavy or clumsy steps, a pronounced gait.*

Cruise: *To walk easily, casually, sail along.*

D

Dance: *To move lightly or rhythmically.*

Dart: *To dash, scoot forward.*

Dash: *To race forward or toward something.*

Dive: *To throw oneself, either from a height or into something.*

Drag: *To pull oneself along.*

Drift: *To move aimlessly, slowly, without clear direction or purpose.*

E

Ease: *To slip along or away, slide.*

Edge: *To move sneakily, inch ones way or to escape.*

Exit: *To depart, leave.*

F

Flit: *To move lightly, quickly, as a bird.*

Float: *To glide or walk lightly, as if on air.*

Flow: *To move smoothly, glide.*

G

Glide: *To move smoothly or easily.*

H

Hike: *To walk some distance or to walk purposefully.*

Hobble: *To walk with a severe limp, as if one's legs are crippled or injured.*

Hurdle: *To leap over.*

Hurry: *To move fast, rush.*

Hurtle: *To throw oneself rapidly or fly through the air out of control.*

Hustle: *To hurry, rush.*

I

Inch: *To move a tiny amount, move slowly.*

J

Jam: *To force oneself into a tight spot, as in hiding.*

Jog: *To run at a leisurely pace.*

Jump: *To leap in the air, jerk or otherwise move in a startled fashion.*

L

Lumber: *To walk heavily, as if one's body weighs a ton.*

M

Maneuver: *To work one's way through, as in getting through or around obstacles.*

March: *To walk in cadence with music or stride with emphasis.*

Meander: *To wander, amble.*

P

Pace: *To walk the same space over and over or to walk with a steady, emphatic rhythm.*

Plod: *To walk in a state of exhaustion or depression.*

Plow: *To go forward regardless of obstacles, force one's way through.*

Pound: *To walk or stride heavily.*

Prance: *To cavort or frolic.*

Promenade: *To parade or walk ceremoniously or haughtily.*

R

Race: *To hurry, run fast.*

Ramble: *To wander, walk without specific direction.*

Retreat: *To back away, flee.*

Roam: *To wander over or through.*

Run: *To move at top speed.*

Rush: *To move quickly or be in a hurry.*

S

Sail: *To walk breezily, easily, glide along.*

Sashay: *To glide or walk suggestively.*

Saunter: *To walk casually, amble.*

Scamper: *To run playfully.*

Scoot: *To move quickly.*

Scurry: *To rush or hurry.*

Shamble: *To walk in a slovenly or clumsy fashion, often associated with being drunk.*

Shove: *To push oneself forward.*

Shuffle: *To slide one's feet, as an elderly person might.*

Sidle: *To ease up to sneakily.*

Skedaddle: *To beat it out of there, run for it, escape.*

Skid: *To slide.*

Skip: *To take short hopping, usually lighthearted steps.*

Skitter: *To dance or bounce erratically across the floor.*

Slide: *To glide.*

Slip: *To lose one's footing or ease through.*

Slither: *To slide or squeeze through.*

Slog: *To struggle forward, as in mud or snow.*

Snake: *To slither through, squeeze.*

Sprint: *To race or dash forward, run quickly.*

Squeeze: *To force through.*

Squirm: *To wiggle or twist forward, usually in a tight space.*

Stagger: *To walk unevenly or uncertainly.*

Step: *To walk or move from one place to another.*

Stomp: *To plant one's feet with intensity or crush something beneath one's feet.*

Storm: *To walk with anger or rage.*

Stride: *To walk with purpose and speed.*

Stroll: *To amble along or walk without hurrying.*

Stumble: *To lose one's footing and stagger or almost fall.*

Swagger: *To walk or stride with bravado or arrogance.*

Sweep: *To move along with grace, to glide across a floor.*

Swish: *To sweep along.*

Swivel: *To turn quickly.*

T

Toddle: *To move with an unsteady gait, like a small child.*

Totter: *To stagger.*

Traipse: *To tramp or plod along.*

Tramp: *To stride with emphasis, stomp.*

Travel: *To cover ground.*

Traverse: *To cover distance.*

Trot: *To hurry along at a half run.*

Trudge: *To walk in a state of exhaustion or reluctantly.*

Tumble: *To fall or to roll.*

W

Waddle: *To move with slow, short steps, shifting from side to side, as a duck.*

Wander: *To walk without purpose or direction, amble.*

Weave: *To shift or step from side to side, as in moving through a crowd or to stagger.*

Wriggle: *To squirm, to squeeze through.*

Alternatives for Look

B

Beam: *To look upon with glowing approval.*

Behold: *To observe or see, usually with reverence.*

Browse: *To glance around.*

D

Direct: *To focus one's attention.*

Discern: *To recognize or note.*

E

Examine: *To study carefully.*

Eye: *To look intensely, often implies disapproval.*

F

Fixate: *To give an intense, lingering look.*

Flash: *To give a brief, pointed look.*

Frown: *To give a disapproving or uncertain look.*

G

Gander: *To take a quick look.*

Gape: *To stare in open mouthed wonder.*

Gawk: *To stare or ogle.*

Gawp: *To stare or ogle.*

Gaze: *To dreamily stare.*

Glance: *To look quickly, superficially.*

Glare: *To stare intently with disapproval.*

Glimpse: *To catch a fleeting look.*

Glower: *To look with an expression of fierce disapproval.*

Goggle: *To stare with wide eyed amazement.*

I

Inspect: *To examine in detail.*

L

Leer: *To hold a lascivious or lustful look.*

Look-see: *To give a once-over.*

N

Notice: *To become aware of.*

O

Observe: *To watch or take note of.*

Ogle: *To stare flirtatiously or impertinently.*

Outface: *To outstare or defy.*

Outstare: *To hold one's gaze until the other relents.*

P

Peek: *To glance quickly and furtively, peep.*

Peep: *To watch secretly or from a hidden place, peek.*

Perceive: *To notice, become aware of.*

Peruse: *To scan or scrutinize.*

Pore over: *To examine microscopically.*

R

Read: *To observe and interpret.*

Regard: *To look with considered interest or feeling.*

Review: *To examine and analyze.*

Rubberneck: *To look gratuitously.*

S

Scan: *To peruse quickly, gather an overall impression.*

Scowl: *To look with angry disapproval.*

Scrutinize: *To study carefully.*

Search: *To look for something.*

See: *To look.*

Seek: *To visually hunt.*

Sight: *To catch a view of.*

Skim: *To review quickly.*

Squint: *To give a sideways glance or to struggle in bright light.*

Stare: *To look intensely or sometimes vaguely, as in a blank stare.*

Study: *To observe and commit to memory.*

Survey: *To do an overall examination.*

V

View: *To take in visually.*

W

Watch: *To observe attentively.*

Wink: *To close an eye and open it, usually done humorously.*

Witness: *To observe personally.*